BE LIKE DAD

DAD

50 Stories for Life & Leadership

BRIAN SANDERS

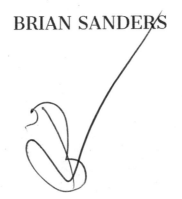

JPL BOOKS

Copyright © 2021 by Brian Sanders

All rights reserved.

No part of this book may be reproduced in any form or by any electronic or mechanical means, including information storage and retrieval systems, without written permission from the author, except for the use of brief quotations in a book review.

FIRST EDITION
ISBN: 978-1-946671-14-1
Library of Congress Control Number: 2021901791
Published by

Disclaimer: The views and opinions expressed in this book are solely those of the author and other contributors. These views and opinions do not necessarily represent those of JPL Books. Please note that JPL Books' publishing style capitalizes certain pronouns in Scripture that refer to the Father, Son, and Holy Spirit, and may differ from some publishers' styles.

To Mom and Dad
with love & gratitude

Brian

CONTENTS

FOREWORD

If you were in our circles or knew my Dad, you never heard the name Marion. (For the record, Dad pronounced it as Mare-ahn.)

It was either Jack, Junior, Dad, Pops, or Poppa.

He entered the world in 1944 and left it in 2018.

He was the son of a sharecropper.

They were poor - dirt poor.

Graduating from Calvin High School in Winn Parish, Louisiana, he joined the Air Force to pursue a better life than the one his parents had.

He would eventually rise to the rank of Master Sergeant when he retired from the military in 1981.

From there, he'd go to work for Haliburton as part of an International Paper mill in Mansfield, Louisiana.

He and Mom were married for over fifty years.

They were wed in Ohio, and I came along while they were stationed in Hawaii.

Their love was strong, and it showed to anyone who knew them.

He was known for his laughter, honesty, integrity, ability to fish, hunt, and tell a good joke.

People often called us twins - both bald with hair on the sides.

The same impatience, humor, and volume are things we shared.

We both had issues with the ability to walk and keep our pants from falling down.

Dad said we were "all gut and no butt."

He was right.

He loved my wife, Kayla, as if she were his own daughter.

Dad taught her to fish, how to bait a hook, and take fish off the line.

These are things she rarely had to do since she was his "Baby Girl."

Dad was my golf instructor, baseball and football coach, and chief inspector of all things competitive that I did.

He played scratch golf, cooked amazing meals, and taught me to hunt.

He tried to pass on his knowledge of bows and arrows, but I never got the hang of it.

Dad was an expert teller of stories and jokes.

He believed in Jesus but would rarely pass through the doors of a church.

We had a thousand conversations about Jesus and the gospel.

He brought everyone to tears at our wedding rehearsal with his speech.

He was proud that he provided a good life for his family, as he should have been.

The book you are about to read is about him.

His stories and what he taught me.

The life he lived and the lessons he taught me about life and leadership.

May you glean wisdom from its pages as I did from the man.

As you read this book and consider the lessons, remember that if you want to be a better leader or simply improve at life, memorize these three words...

BE LIKE DAD

Brian Sanders

INTRODUCTION

Dear Dad,

I wish you could hold this book and read it.

However, you left us in August of 2018 after a two month battle with cancer.

In some strange way, I think you know about this book.

It won't shock me if Jesus has a way for you to read it.

In these pages, you'll read how you influenced me.

These stories and memories are the stuff that comprise the moral and leadership fiber that forms me today.

Any success I have had as a husband, human, and leader is because of you.

Dad, your influence is evident in every area of my life.

And so, I want to share those lessons and stories with others so they can benefit from the greatest man I ever knew....you.

I'm thankful for you, your influence, integrity, conversations, and experiences we've had over the years.

Thanks for believing in me and never telling me I was stupid or a failure, even when I may have embarrassed you.

Thanks for the unconditional love and always accepting me back after some stupid bumble I had made.

Miss ya.

Love ya.

A grateful son —

Brian

1. INNOVATE AND HAVE SOME FUN

The house they lived in reflected their poverty.

My grandfather was a sharecropper in Ouachita Parish, Louisiana. The home they lived in was provided by the owner of the land that my grandfather farmed.

You could lay in bed, look to the ceiling, and see stars in the gaps of the roof.

The house raised off the ground enough that chickens walked underneath.

The floor had cracks — major ones.

That led the boy to an idea.

His mom took a cane pole, tied a string to it, and used corn for bait.

There he sat, in the living room, fishing.

He'd drop the line through the cracks in the floor, and he'd feel a tug.

You guessed it…instead of trying to pull in a fish…he'd "caught" a chicken.

That little boy was my Dad.

As a boy, Dad was fighting a toothache. To help him pass the time and hopefully ignore the pain, he fished for chickens.

There's a lesson in that for me.

My grandparents innovated.

Instead of just putting him in bed and fighting a toddler who was in pain, they gave him a task, and it was fun.

Think about it…he could sit on the floor where his mom could watch him, all while he did something that made him laugh and giggle.

Innovation.

Perhaps…just perhaps…your organization is facing some painful tasks. Projects that have to be done, but they cause a little pain.

Take a lesson from my Dad…fish for chickens.
Make the task fun.
Turn it into a contest.
Maybe form teams with various team members, and put gift cards on the line.

Whatever you do, innovate.

Don't just expect people to do tasks and projects, especially laborious ones, without mumbling and grumbling.

Team members will require a reframing of tasks so they can see them from a new perspective — one that will give purpose and fun.

Take a few moments today.

Gather the team.

Brainstorm for a few on how to make the projects and tasks fun.

Generate ideas that will motivate them through the tough and tedious.

Your idea may not be fishing for chickens... but it needs to generate a smile and a laugh.

Be like Dad...innovate and have some fun.

2. BE EARLY AND SET THE EXAMPLE

Mom and Dad were flying to Roanoke to visit us.

Their flight left Shreveport at 10 a.m.

What time does Dad have them at the airport?

    6 a.m.

Yes, Dad and Mom were at the airport four hours before the flight was to leave.

Mind you, the Shreveport airport has a total of six gates. Atlanta, it's not.

If Dad had a meeting, he showed up at least fifteen minutes early.

It was a cardinal sin, and inexcusable, to be late.

Dad's punctuality wasn't a result of some superior beating down on him.

He was a leader in the Air Force.

After the military, he took a job with Brown and Root. He led an electrical maintenance team at a paper mill in Louisiana.

Understand this,

> Dad wasn't following an example, he was setting it.

As the leader, don't just be on time, be early.

You're showing the other party great respect by communicating they are worth even MORE of your time.

What does being late say to those your meeting?

> You're more important.
> Your time is more valuable than theirs.
> Whatever it is you are dealing with is more critical than what they are trying to solve.
> You are superior.

These are things you do NOT want to communicate.

Once you're in the meeting —

> Be present.
> Don't look at your watch.
> Give them your full attention.
> Make sure the room knows how much time you have for the meeting.
> While you're there…nothing else interrupts the meeting.

Be early.
Show respect.
Be present.
Never be late.

Do these things, and you'll be a better leader.

Your team will respect you and know they can count on you when it comes to meetings.

If you ever met Dad, you knew he walked at a pace of fifty mph.

Why?

He didn't want to be late!

Be like Dad…be early and set the example.

3. STAND UP AGAINST INJUSTICE

I worked at a small radio station in our hometown of Coushatta, Louisiana.

When school ended, I'd speed off to host the afternoon show.

A high school friend and I worked there. We got in an argument like high schoolers do.

Well, the midday guy heard us arguing.

Remember, I'm sixteen-years-old.

The midday guy is thirty-five or forty.

He storms through the door, walks up to me, gets within an inch of my face, and begins to yell.

He pulls back his fist and says, "If you ever argue with her again, you'll deal with me. She's like a sister to me."

All I could say was, "We're friends. Friends disagree and argue."

The whole time she's trying to calm him down so he won't hit me.

The midday guy continues to yell, fists clenched and threatening to put me on the floor.

No one else was at the station.

No one.

Emotions finally calm down.

My shift ends, and I go home.

Dad asks, "How was work?"

I tell him what happened.

OH. MY. WORD.

Dad goes to the phone and calls his friend, Sam.

I hear, "Can you be here in five minutes? We have a situation to handle."

Sure enough, within five minutes, Sam comes screeching into our driveway.

Dad looks at me and says, "Get in the truck. We're gonna take care of this."

Dad grabs a shotgun and puts it in the gun rack in the truck's back window.

And now, Sam, Dad, and I are in a truck headed to Hickory Grove Road.

It was then it dawned on me.

> We're headed to the house of the midday
> guy....and Dad has a gun...Sam is with
> us....and Sam has a gun.

Dad tells Sam the story.

He responds with, "Jack, we can't stand for this.
This man has to be shown he can't push kids
around."

> It's like I'm in the twilight zone.
> Is this really happening?

Dad makes a turn.

Stops in a driveway.

He leaves the truck running.

Dad gets out of the truck and grabs the gun.

I'm thinking, "Is he going to kill him? Is this really
going to happen?"

Sam gets out of the truck.

Me? I'm sitting in the truck wondering if I'm going
to be part of a crime scene.

Dad starts to yell the midday guy's name.

> "Bob!! Bob!! Bob!!"
> (I've changed the guy's name to protect his
> identity.)

About that time, the door opens, and Bob steps on the porch.

Dad continues to yell,

> "Bob, I'm Jack Sanders. My son is Brian. Today, you screamed at my son. You got in his face. You clenched a fist and made him believe you were going to hit him. Let me be clear what will happen the next time…"

Dad points the shotgun in the air and pulls the trigger.

The sound of the shotgun echoes through the woods.

Dad then says,

> "Do I make myself clear? Do you understand?"

Bob yells back, "But sir, you don't understand…"

Dad fires off another shot to the air, then yells,

> "Am I clear?"

Bob exclaims, "Yes, sir. Very clear."

Dad and Sam got back in the truck.

We went back home like nothing had happened.

What's the leadership lesson?

Defend what's right.

As a leader, you must defend your team, the culture, the mission, vision, and the organization as a whole.

Let's be clear...don't grab a gun and scare people into submission.

But Dad's overall example is worthy.

He handled an injustice.

Leaders must do that, as well.

Someone develops a sour attitude and begins to impact the culture...address it.

Team members begin undermining the mission or vision by mocking it, saying it isn't important... handle it instantly.

If that spreads, your organization will develop a cancer that could kill it.

The longer you allow issues to linger, the likelihood those spoiling the culture will think it's okay to undercut the organization and your leadership

Handle the issue privately.

If it spreads, then handle it publicly.
If needed, fire the person.

Be like Dad...stand up against injustices. (Just don't use a gun to do so.)

For the record, "Bob" never raised his voice at me again. Imagine that.

4. KEEP LEARNING

If you ever had the chance to watch television with Dad, you likely heard this coming from the speaker, "And now...the antelope grazes without realizing the danger that lurks just beyond the hedge..."

Or you might have heard, "Theories abound about black holes—their power to create and destroy. Do they lead to another dimension, or do they simply destroy into a vast nothingness?"

Dad loved to learn.

He wasn't a lover of books, but he loved learning.

Any kind of nature show focused on how animals live and interact, he'd watch every episode.

Documentaries about space and creation, he would watch the whole thing.

Dad was an avid golfer and bass fisherman. He'd watch golf and fishing tournaments, not for enjoyment, but to learn.

He'd watch golf to learn how and when they broke their wrists during the swing, when they shifted their weight, and where to strike the ball. He'd watch them shape shots so the ball would move at their desire.

After watching, Dad would go to the range and practice, practice, practice.

He'd watch the Bassmaster Tournament Series on ESPN.

Why?

He wanted to watch HOW they fished. Was there a new technique? Is there a new bait that is attracting the fish? How were the pros using technology to read the shape of the land and understand how the fish move?

Dad loved to learn…especially if it made him better at things he enjoyed doing.

President Truman once said that "Not all readers are leaders, but all leaders are readers."

His point?

Leaders love to learn.

In today's world, you can learn through books, podcasts, audiobooks, TED talks, YouTube, and by simply Googling your interest.

There's no excuse for a leader not to be learning.

The ways in which leaders can better themselves are almost innumerable.

Make yourself better.

> **Learn.**
> **Practice.**
> **Learn some more.**
> **Practice some more.**

Books are my preferred method. They force me to focus and help my brain stop thinking about the stresses and ideas I could be experiencing.

Dad watched all those shows because he knew he didn't know everything.

He was humble enough to recognize the skills of others and how they could better him.

Want to be a better leader?

> Read books about leadership.
> Listen to lectures.
> Find some TED Talks.
> Be a student of your passion.

Be a student long enough, and you'll eventually become an expert.

Be like Dad...keep learning.

5. TAKE A CHANCE

Decisions are like drinks at Starbucks.

They come in three sizes - tall, grande, and venti.

This decision was a venti.

Dad was thirty-seven.

He had served twenty years in the Air Force.

Should he stay in for another twenty or get out now, take his retirement, and have a second career?

He'd sit at the dining room table with a pad of paper and a pen. You'd see a list of pros and cons.

At the time of this massive decision, we lived in Alexandria, Louisiana, at England Air Force Base.

I was thirteen years old, and I remember asking Dad what he was doing.

He said,

"Trying to make a decision. Do I stay in the military, or do I get out and go for a second career? This isn't as easy as the first time."

I asked, "The first time?"

Dad replied,

"When I was eighteen, I made the decision to leave home and go in the military. I had watched your grandfather follow a mule and plow land that wasn't his. He made a good life for me, your aunt, and grandmother -- but I knew there had to be more. I didn't want to follow a mule all day in the burning hot sun. I knew there had to be more."

That was the extent of the conversation. Dad went back to his list. Two columns filled with words as he tried to weigh the risks and rewards.

He could stay in the safety of the military.

Housing was provided.
The community was safe.
There was a hospital right on base.
We had friends who were more like family.

But Dad didn't stay.

At thirty-seven years old, he opted to retire from the Air Force and enter the private sector.

He landed as the leader of a paper mill maintenance team just south of Shreveport, Louisiana.

Mom and Dad bought a house, and the rest was history.

Later in life, I asked Dad why he made that choice. Why did he leave the safety and comfort of the Air Force and decide to have a second career?

His answer?

> "I had to look beyond the now. If I had stayed, I'd be getting out of the Air Force at age fifty-seven or so. It would be easier to get a job as a thirty-seven-year-old than a fifty-seven-year-old. That one piece of information made me take the leap."

For leaders, so many lessons here.

First, plan for the future.

You can't just look at the here and now.

> Or, as Dad used to say, "You must look beyond the nose on your face."

For a leader, if you make that decision --

> Play it out to the end. How will it impact your organization, cash flow, and team members five years from now? Ten years from now? Twenty years from now?

Second, some decisions are gut calls.

You can have all the data in the world and still not be sure.

In the end, Dad took a chance.

The choice he made was still a risk.

There was no guarantee he would be successful, but he knew he wouldn't be if he didn't try.

Some situations require you to consider all the data but then take the leap.

Third, leaders remember the past.

Dad leaped once before. He left home at eighteen and went into the Air Force. Granted, the leap wasn't as large. He wasn't leaving the possibility of a great future. But all the same, he still leaped.

As you encounter major decisions today, remember the ones you made in the past.

> It'll give you the perspective and courage you need to move forward.

The 100-foot cliff jump isn't as scary when you remember you successfully made the 75-foot dive.

Dad had created a new life once before. That gave him some confidence he could do it again.

You've launched new products in the past. You can do it again.

Sure, there may be more at stake this time, but you have the experience to navigate it. Your history says you do.

Finally, you never know what you're capable of until you take the chance.

Dad could have stayed in the velvet prison of the Air Force.

> All the comforts.
> All the security.

He left it all to create a new future.

As a leader, you should have a dream -- one that scares you.

You'll never achieve it just sitting there.

You must take the chance.

Failure gives you stories to tell and lessons learned.
Success gives you an opportunity to chase new dreams.

Be like Dad…take a chance.

6. PRACTICE, PRACTICE, PRACTICE

What golf game I have, I owe to Dad.

He was my teacher, coach, and best playing partner ever.

"You're breaking your wrists too early."

"Hit the back of the ball first. Don't hit the ground."

"You should feel your weight shift from one foot to the other, and that gives your swing the power to propel the ball."

"Son, keep your head down."

I've heard those phrases a million times.

Early in my golf game, I had a notorious habit of picking up my head on the backswing.

This would absolutely drive Dad up a wall.

Being a natural innovator, Dad stood next to me and put the grip end of a golf club on my head while he held the other end of the club.

Amazingly, I kept my head down.

We didn't do that just once or twice.

I took at least 50 to 100 practice swings with that on my head.

We'd go to the golf course and get buckets of balls and just practice.

I'd beg to play.

"Let's hit the course, Dad!"

Nope.

He was adamant that I had to learn the fundamentals before spreading my wings on an actual course.

Eventually, I got on the course, and we'd play golf as much as possible.

As we played, he was always the coach. He'd see something in my swing and try to help me fix it.

While in college, Dad drove down, and we played a round at the course the university owned.

My favorite golfer of all time is Curtis Strange.

I made the quip to Dad, "I'd love to be as good as Curtis Strange." Without hesitating, Dad said,

"Then practice. I know he's your favorite

golfer, so I did a little research. Curtis hits 500 balls in the morning, then does bunker practice, and then hits the putting green for 45 minutes. It's only then that he goes on the course and plays 18 holes. After he plays, he returns to the practice tee and hits 500 more balls and then works on his chipping game."

Dad's point?

If you want Curtis Strange's game, you must put in the time and practice that Curtis does. Some of you reading this want to be the next Steve Jobs, Jack Welch, or Oprah.

Hit the practice tee.

What do I mean?

You must do the little things now so you can handle big things later.

Is the team asking you to write blogs?

Practice writing. Choose a topic and just write.

More video?

Get in front of a camera and practice trying to be natural. What head movements work and which ones don't?

Worried you won't be able to make decisions?

> Start making small ones.
> Rearrange workloads.
> Put people in the right seats.
> Make financial choices.

Whether you realize it or not, those small decisions will be the practice you'll need for bigger decisions later in your leadership career.

There's no shortcut to success.
You must put in the time and effort.

Be like Dad...practice, practice, and practice some more.

7. LEARN TO TELL A STORY

The roar of his laughter could be heard a mile away, and that roar usually followed a story he told.

To know my Dad was to know a storyteller.

If he was in a room, he was the center -- and not just the center -- he owned the room.

Story after story would flow -- ones that were embarrassing to him but made you love him even more.

He would tell serious stories that pierced your soul and left you considering how to change something about yourself, as well as funny stories with laughter at the end.

People would visit just to hear Dad's stories.

Most importantly, people left changed.

Dad wouldn't tell people how to be a better fisherman; he told a story that illustrated the point.

With his employees at the paper mill, Dad wouldn't just tell them what to do; he illustrated it with a story.

And this is the key to Dad's storytelling.

By explaining the why in story form, anyone who heard a story left better because of it.

People remember them.
They recount the truth within the story.
One never forgets the storyteller.
A story unites us.

Don't just tell your team what to do.

Illustrate it with a story.
Your team will never forget.

Simply communicating rules can create rebellion. After all, look at the history of the human race.

Stories build community, connection, and create momentum.

Told with the right tone and passion, a story can motivate us.

Be like Dad…learn to tell a story.

8. PLAY WHERE YOU CAN WIN

Focus on your strengths.

That's a famous lesson from the one and only John Maxwell.

For me, before Maxwell…there was Dad.

As a kid, Dad would say, "Play the games you can win."

Dad did just that.

My Dad was an avid golfer.

He'd get home from working a long day and go to the practice range.

He was good -- very good.

He'd often shoot under par.

The fellas at the country club always wanted Dad on their team when it came time to play.

Dad was also a great bass fisherman.

How good was he?

When the Pros came to town for a major fishing tournament, they'd call Dad and want him to go with them. They wanted to see where he fished, how he fished, what he fished, and when he fished.

They knew if they could replicate what "Mr. Jack" was doing, they'd stand a good chance of winning.

You'd never see Dad participating in a football game or soccer.

Why?

Dad played in the arenas where he could win.

In other words…

Dad focused on his strengths.

At Dad's memorial service, one of his best friends came to me and said, "Your Dad only played where he could win. If he couldn't be the best, your Dad didn't mess with it."

He was right.

There's a lesson there for leaders.

Play where you can win.

Where are you strong?

Let that be your wheelhouse.

Where are you weak?

Be honest with that, and hire people to support you in those areas.

You can't be good at everything.

It's impossible.

If you're great at vision casting but grow weary in the tedious tasks, then hire a talented project manager who can guide projects.

You can't just cast a vision.

There must be doing and accomplishing.

Stay in your lane, and you'll find success will be a tad easier.

Be like Dad…play where you can win.

9. SHARE YOUR WORLD

He'd come home, put his keys on the table, sit down to a dinner that Mom cooked, and begin to talk.

She never had to ask.

He just talked.

Dad would begin sharing about his day.

> "Well, the number three machine went down today. Had to send Jim up to the powerhouse to reconfigure the fuses…and while he was there we got another call…"

Mom would listen.

Dad would just walk her through the events of the day.

You'd hear her ask questions, and he'd answer.

On other days, Dad would talk, and Mom would ask a question.

Dad would quip, "Let me finish!"

Mom would dart back, "I'm just asking a question!!"

He'd bring home a massive spreadsheet with names.

Dad was trying to figure out a schedule for a major upcoming project at the mill.

He'd sit down at the table, pencil in hand, and begin to stare at that paper.

Write a little...think...write a little...think...wash, rinse and repeat.

As he did, he'd talk to Mom about it.

> "I'm thinking about putting Roy here for six hours so that I can put Steve over there."

Dad was sharing his world.

As a leader, he knew he couldn't keep all this stuff bottled up.

A leader needs someone they can share life with.

> The ups and downs.
> The doubts and questions.
> The celebrations and the crises.

Dad knew he couldn't do leadership alone.

It was simply too much.

So he talked to Mom.

This helped Dad's stress level by having someone in his corner who empathized with his stress and burden.

It gave him a sounding board. As he talked to Mom, he had a judgment-free zone where he could vent about others and confess his own faults.

He also knew there was someone ALWAYS in his corner.

Mom would defend him no matter the story or situation Dad shared.

> A leader needs that because there are days they feel very, very alone.

Dad intentionally talked about his job and the stress that surrounded it.

Mom never had to beg him to share.

> Want to last as a leader?

Share your world with someone.
Talk. Vent. Listen.

Be like Dad…share your world.

10. MAKE THE TEAM A FAMILY

It had to be 4 a.m.

The clanging of metal on metal woke me up.

I stumbled to the door and saw Dad putting stuff in the back of his pick up.

"Dad, it's 4 a.m. -- what in the world?"

> "I had to load the fish fryer, gas tank, and so on. I'm doing a fish fry for my crew at the mill."

Dad would fry the fish. Mom would stay home and make all the sides -- fries, hushpuppies, onions, and coleslaw.

She'd then drive to the mill and deliver to Dad.

Why did Dad do this?

> Dad knew that a team that plays well together works well together.

He was building community among his
team.

They'd swap stories about fishing and hunting
and then tell jokes and make fun of each other.

All of this happened over a great meal.

Dad knew that great conversations happen
over good meals, and great conversations
are the foundational building blocks of a
highly functioning team.

That's why Dad went to all that trouble.

He knew it would strengthen relationships and
lead to a better team.

Spend time with your team making memories and
having great conversations.

Meals are a great way to achieve this.
Talk about family.
Share some of your favorite stories.
You'll see friendships start to be born.
Trust will strengthen.

You can't just be the leader twenty-four hours
a day.

Be a person.
Have some real conversations.
Share some laughs.
Make fun of yourself.

The team needs to see there's a real person behind the title and confidence.

> Your team will be better because of it.
> We want to identify with our leaders.
> See them as people we can become.

Slow down and build relationships.

Be like Dad…make the team a family.

11. TAKE THE CHANCE

Crawfish are a big deal in Louisiana.

Dad was still in the Air Force and stationed in Alexandria, Louisiana.

I must have been in the fifth or sixth grade.

We had been talking about how good a fried crawfish Po-Boy would be. (It's a sandwich on French bread.)

Dad announces, "Let's solve this problem!"

He goes to the shed.

He starts putting stuff in the back of his pick-up and then informs Mom that we'll be back soon.

We both crawl in the truck.

Dad tells me we have crawfish nets in the back of the truck, and we're going to catch some, fry them up, and have sandwiches.

But to do that…we have to catch the crawfish.

Dad stops at a grocery store and buys raw chicken.

We arrive at a pond.

Dad cuts up the chicken into small pieces, ties them to the bottom of the nets, and sets them in the shallows of the pond. Three metal prongs, making the shape of a triangle, connect the net and stick up from the water. He has a long pole that reaches out in the water, allowing him to pick up the nets without having to get in the water and get wet.

He sets at least ten nets. And then we wait.

We're there thirty minutes when Dad says, "Oh crap."

Then I see it.

A water moccasin, a very poisonous snake, is swimming toward the traps.

First, Dad doesn't want the snake to get near us.

Second, he doesn't want the snake in the traps eating the chicken because there goes our bait, and we get no crawfish.

Third, we just don't like snakes.

I remember it like it was yesterday.

Dad was a famed baseball pitcher in high school in Calvin, Louisiana.

I knew he had been good, but not that good...

What does he do?

He finds a rock about half the size of your hand.

The snake gets closer and closer.

Dad does the wind-up, delivers the pitch...and bam!!

The rock hits the snake squarely on the head.

Perfect pitch!!

The snake rolled over dead.

He takes the long pole, fishes the snake out of the water, and cuts off the head with a machete that he carried in a box in his truck. (It's a Louisiana thing. Don't ask.)

I was amazed.

"Dad, that was incredible. I knew you were a good baseball pitcher. But one shot, and you nailed that snake."

Dad responds with,

> "I took a chance and made the right shot. Don't be too impressed. I just had to take the chance. If I had missed, I would have kept trying with more rocks."

There's the leadership lesson.

You have to take a chance.

You may not achieve victory on the first try. Very few attempts ever do.

But keep trying.

So what if you fail?

You discovered a way that won't work.

Keep clawing your way to your goal.

Sometimes the odds will force your hand.

The snake forced Dad to act.

New competition, new platforms, or a change in how the product is made may push you to act.

Be nimble enough to make the move.

Dad could have said, "Well, we're done for the day. That's a failed attempt."

But he didn't.

And neither should you!

Be like Dad…take the chance.

For the record, the Po-Boys were excellent.

12. POSITION PEOPLE TO HAVE A SHOT

Andrews Air Force Base is located in Washington, DC, and that's where Dad was stationed.

To know my parents is to know they love both professional and college football.

I must have been nine or ten years old, and my Mom was the world's biggest fan of Washington DC's football team.

> She was not just a fan of the team, but their famed quarterback, Joe Theisman.

I could be a block away from the house on a Sunday afternoon and hear my Mom hollering at the television.

A friend would say, "Hey guys, there's Brian's Mom cheering on her team!!"

Dad knew Mom loved her team. He also knew she liked Joe Theisman.

Theisman was making an appearance at a local car dealership.

Dad decides to take Mom.

We walk into the showroom on the evening of Theisman's appearance.

The place was packed.

A stage has been built in the center of the room, surrounded by people and new cars.

Dad and I are standing in the back.

Mom has eased her way to the middle of the crowd. She wants a good view.

Theisman says a few words, and the crowd applauds.

Unknown to us, he picks up a large box full of mini footballs.

He reaches into the box and begins to spiral footballs out to the crowd.

After doing that three or four times, he takes handfuls and begins tossing them to his fans.

A football is tossed in the direction of my Mom.

She jumps. Her hands are in the air.

As she's in the air, somehow, her feet and legs go forward.

She catches the ball, but instead of landing on her feet…she lands directly on her bottom.

Theisman sees all of it — the whole scene.

He leans over the stage, makes eye contact with Mom, and just smiles and giggles.

In the back, Dad is doubled over with tears running down his cheeks from laughter.

Mom picks herself up, walks toward Dad, and says, "Go ahead. Laugh. But I got a football."

Dad says, "And you made a memory for old Joe."

Everyone laughed.

But Mom can teach us a leadership lesson.

Don't worry about what the crowd thinks of you when you go for the goal.

Who cares if people were laughing or Joe Theisman never forgot her…she got what she wanted.

Many leaders get frozen in place until everything is right -- the image, the process, and the team.

Take a cue from Mom, jump for it anyway.

Who cares if you end up on your bottom? You might just come up with the ball.

What you'll discover is that leaders mostly bumble and fumble their way to the goal.

It's a relentless series of ups and downs as we march toward the mission and vision.

Who cares if you land on your feet just as long as you eventually come up with the ball.

Be like Mom…jump for the goal!

Also, be like Dad…position your people to have a shot at the ball.

13. ENCOURAGE
YOUR TEAM

His name was Jeff Chambers.

He was my sixth-grade arch-nemesis.

He was athletic.

I was not.

He could do fractions.

I could not.

He towered over me by at least a foot.

I was as wide as he was tall.

On this particular day, the tension exploded.

Yep, two sixth-graders fought.

In a side yard by his house, we tumbled and tossed with fists flying.

I surrendered in defeat.

Walking home, I wondered what my Dad's reaction would be.

Like a scene from a movie, Dad was at the door when I got home.

"Boy, what happened?"

My lip was bleeding.

My chin was cut.

One eye was swollen.

I explained that Jeff had beaten me up, and I had lost the fight.

In his best authoritative voice, he proclaimed,

> "Well, son, climb back on that horse. Go back to his house, knock on his door, and when he comes outside,…whip his butt!" (Let me be clear…Dad didn't say "butt.")

So, I left our house rallied with new confidence, and marched to the Chambers' home.

I knock on the door.

Jeff answers.

And right there…in the front yard…he wins again.

I go home, and Dad sees me.

I'll never forget what he says,

> "Well, son, Dad gave you bad advice that
> time. Come here, let's get ya cleaned up
> before ya momma gets home."

Even as I type the story, I'm laughing.

There are some leadership lessons in this story.

First, Dad was right.

We must face our fears and battle them.

Even if they knock us down, we must rise back up
and square off again.

Leaders don't stay in the dirt in defeat.

Churchill said, "Success consists of going from
failure to failure without loss of enthusiasm."

In his own way, that's the lesson my Dad
taught me.

Success wasn't staying down.

Even though Chambers did knock me back down
again, at least he knew I was willing to face him.

Second, Dad was willing to admit he made a
mistake.

That's key for leaders.

Instead of justifying why he sent me back to Jeff's
house, Dad owned the decision.

This is hard for leaders to do.

We want to be seen as right, flawless, all-knowing, and visionary.

In reality, we need to be seen as resilient, battle-worn, but unwilling to quit.

We must let the team see us as human — riddled with flaws and making mistakes but moving forward trying to do things right.

Be like Dad…encourage your team to face their fears…not once, not twice…but over and over again.

14. KNOW THE RISKS

Most of our significant conversations happened on a boat with fishing rods in our hands.

That's just the way we rolled.

If the Red River in Coushatta, Louisiana, could talk, I'm sure it could recount a million conversations I've had with Dad.

With the sound of a fishing line going through a reel, I asked, "When you went to Vietnam, were you afraid?"

His foot navigating the trolling motor, he said, "Yes. Yes, I was afraid, but I knew the cost."

The phrase hit me oddly, so I had to follow up.

"What do you mean you knew the cost?" I asked.

"Son, before anyone enlists in the military, they have to make a choice. Are they willing to pay the price? Let's face it. The reason America has a military is to win wars. Others will tell you it's to keep the peace and so on, but really the military is there to win wars."

"Gotcha. I'm tracking."

"If you know that, and it's pretty obvious, then you must decide if you're willing to take the risk. The risk that you could die. Yes, the military provides pay, housing, medical, and great benefits, but there's a big risk for all of that. You must be comfortable with that risk before you sign the dotted line and commit your life. Yes, I was afraid, but I also knew the risk and was willing to take it."

That's a conversation I'll never forget, and it's one that leaders should note.

Know the risk.

Before agreeing to the merger or launching a new product line, have you considered all the changes?

Do you have a list of the risks?

Or, are you so blinded by an opportunity that you can't see the price that'll have to be paid?

You're considering expanding the team. That's a good thing!

Before pulling the trigger, have you done your analysis?

> What are the costs?
> How about the benefits?
> Have you considered how the personalities will interact with each other?
> What's the person's role?
> Is there enough work to keep him/her busy?

The military is there to win wars.

Your organization exists to fulfill a mission and a vision.

To achieve them, are you willing to pay the price?

Be like Dad…know the risks and be willing to pay them.

15. CONSTANTLY ENCOURAGE AND COACH

"Now watch me…pay attention…this is how you bait the hook…you begin with the worm."

"Hold the gun to your shoulder. Hold it firmly because it'll kick."

"Swing the golf club for accuracy, not distance. It doesn't matter if you hit the ball 300 yards and end up in the water. You'd rather be 220 yards and in the fairway."

"Son, when you swing the ax -- aim for the middle of the piece of wood. That will help create even pieces of firewood."

"Never forget, when you get behind the wheel of the vehicle, that everyone outside the car becomes an idiot. Drive with that in mind."

Those are things my Dad said to me.

He didn't just say them once.

He repeated them over and over and over.

Why?

I'll never forget what he said, "Boy, I tell you all this so you can be the best. You don't want to be an average fisherman, hunter, or golfer. You want to be the best."

That was Dad.

Not only did he want to be the best at whatever he did, but he also wanted his son to be as well.

And so he coached -- constantly.

Even though he had taught me to hit a golf ball, he never stopped trying to help me improve my swing.

He taught me how to bait a hook, read a depth finder, and understand how the color of the water should determine the color of the lure you use.

He did all that -- but he wanted me to be better.

That's leadership.

He saw potential in me.

He knew I could be and do better.

Dad didn't just bear down on me to improve.

He'd brag on good shots, fish caught, and wood cut, but he'd also coach me to be better.

As a leader, you must do the same with your team.

You don't just teach the basics and walk away.

Leadership is more than just equipping people for the journey...

It's encouraging them so they make it to the finish line.

It's helping them improve their skill sets, so things that used to take an hour now only take fifteen minutes.

The leader explains the why not just the how.

You must connect their work to a cause, so team members develop a passion for what they do.

Be like Dad...constantly encourage and coach.

16. BE PATIENT AND IMPATIENT

My Dad was not a patient man.

Life was a series of events meant to be conquered.

When out to eat, and Dad was done with the meal, he'd pay the bill and stand up. It was a signal that it was time to move on to the next thing.

A store was not a place to visit.

You go with a purpose and accomplish said purpose.

Dad would often proclaim, "Don't lollygag around. Let's get what we came for and get rolling."

(This is also why Mom would go shopping alone. She didn't want to be rushed.)

If there were a project to be done, it would haunt Dad.

This pressure would invade him.

My wife, Kayla, and I took Mom and Dad to Pigeon Forge one year.

We rented a cabin and had tickets to Dollywood.

Mom slipped and ended up with a hairline fracture in her foot.

She didn't want to slow down the family vacation, so she pushed us all to Dollywood.

We had concerns, but here we all were at the amusement park.

Dad secured a wheelchair for Mom.

If you've never been to Dollywood, give me a moment to set the stage.

It's built in the mountains of East Tennessee, so the park is very hilly. It's up and down.

Also, there are wheelchair lanes.

The general public is to walk in one lane while those in wheelchairs and scooters have their own lane.

Mom is in a wheelchair with one foot without a shoe and wrapped in a bandage.

Dad is behind her, pushing the wheelchair.

How do I accurately describe the scene?

He wasn't just pushing the wheelchair.

Dad was more like a jet engine behind the wheelchair.

Kayla and I would look up, and Mom had her arms out, trying to maintain balance, screaming her lungs out with, "Jack!! Slow down!!"

Dad hit a downward slope and took advantage of the momentum.

He wasn't jogging, but he had a good trot going.

Mom looked over at us and yelled, "Kids! Help!!"

All we could do was laugh.

People were parting like the Red Sea.

Mothers were scooping up their children, while others on scooters were scattering to get out of the way.

They arrived at a park bench where Dad sat with Mom parked by his side.

"Are you trying to kill me?" Mom yelled.

"I was trying to get from here to there, and I got us from here to there," Dad replied.

I said, "Dad -- there are wheelchair and scooter lanes. You can use those and take your time."

He replied, "They're too slow. Folks need to make way for those of us trying to have fun."

We all laughed.

Patience and impatience both serve a leader well.

As a leader, you must be patient as you march toward the mission and vision.

You are to be impatient with the tasks and projects that will accomplish the mission and vision.

If your goal is to be the industry leader in quality lawnmowers, you must be patient as your story spreads and the brand is built.

However, you must be impatient when it comes to the quality of the product.

Be patient with the growth of your team.

Be impatient with the things that will grow them.

Be like Dad...be patient in some areas and impatient in others.

17. TAKE PRIDE IN WHAT
YOU DO

The older Dad got, the more obsessed he became
with his yard.

> "Boy, that yard has grown so much in the
> last two days. I have to mow it again."

But the grass hadn't really grown that much. The
issue? He wanted his yard to look the best of all
those in the neighborhood.

At the same time, you would find Dad washing
his bass boat and sometimes even waxing it.

> "That river water puts grime and muck all
> over it. Have to keep her looking good."

Then we'd go down to the dock to launch for a
day of fishing, and you'd hear someone say, "Mr.
Jack, your boat looks good!"

> And that was the payoff.

Dad may not have had the best boat in the river, but he did want to have the best-looking one.

He often called this "taking pride in what you do."

If you had ownership in a project or thing, then it would reveal itself in how you cared for it.

Leaders take ownership.

You may not own the business where you work.

But leaders treat it as if they own it.

You'll see them taking out the trash, washing the vehicles, setting up protocols to protect the business transactions, and so on.

Be wary of anyone who says, "It isn't my business" or "That isn't my job."

And treating the organization as if it's all on you.

A key component of effective leadership is ownership.

Dad believed that his yard and bass boat were reflections of him.

The organization you lead and serve is a reflection of you.

Does it show that you take pride in it?

Would a brief visit from others illustrate that you take ownership?

Get your hands dirty.
Do the menial things.
You'll be a better leader because of it.

Be like Dad…take pride in what you do.

18. ADDRESS WHAT YOU WANT CHANGED

The river was just a short walk from their house.

For a family that had a four-year-old, you learned to keep a watchful eye on the toddler because the river could spell a horrible ending.

On this particularly hot summer day, he escaped the eye of my grandmother.

She couldn't remember the last time she had seen him.

Dreadful thoughts entered her mind.

She ran out the front door and looked at the ground.

Footprints. Where were his footprints?

Even though they were near a river in North Louisiana, the grass didn't grow well, so it left the dusty ground exposed.

She found the signs of little feet and began to follow the tracks.

They were headed right toward the river.

Her heart raced.

Panic filled her mind.

And then she saw him sitting under a tree with his dad.

The toddler, my Dad, left the house without telling his mother and decided to go to the fields with his dad.

From the tree they were sitting under, she broke off a small branch and hurriedly plucked all the leaves.

"Young man, get up from there!"

My grandfather looked at his wife, Pauline, and said, "What's the problem?"

"Junior left the house without telling me. I thought he went to the river, and he could have drowned."

From that tree all the way to the front door of their shanty house, a switch would stripe his legs. With each swing of the branch, my grandmother would say to my Dad, "If you ever leave this house again without telling me where you're going…"

When my grandfather came home from the fields, he said, "Did you notice the boy's footsteps? Coming to the fields, his tracks were very close together. Leaving the fields, they were far apart."

Grandma replied, "That's because I had a switch on him."

The lesson stuck.

Even as a grown man, my dad would tell his mother where he was going when he left their house.

Correction should change behavior.

As a leader, you want improvement and change.

The coaching and correcting you give have a purpose.

Your desire is that the team leave differently than when they arrived.

Most days, you lead change by inspiration.

Other days, there's candor that spotlights specific changes that must be made.

No matter the method, you need to look for a change in footprints.

They are to work and live differently after coaching.

Don't get a switch and chase workers around the office — you'll be in endless meetings with HR and lawyers and be on the front page of the local paper.

But, be like Dad's mom, my Grandma Pauline...know the behavior you want to see changed and address it.

19. BE BRAVE BUT
CONSIDER NEXT STEPS

This story will prove we are from Louisiana.

We were at my grandfather's house in Winn Parish.

A friend of the family brought some baby alligators by the house for everyone to see.

There were three small gators, probably no more than eight to ten inches in length.

They were in the back of a truck where everyone could lean over and view.

Dad couldn't stand it.

He took a stick, cornered one, and with that stick held down its mouth while he grabbed it from behind, holding its mouth shut.

With the gator secured in Dad's strong hands, everyone approached to pet the critter.

Again, this is how we passed the time in Louisiana.

Off to the right was a white styrofoam cooler that someone had put holes in for air.

Dad lowered the gator into that cooler and put the lid on.

No one, and I mean no one, thought to tape or secure the lid.

Within sixty seconds, that gator came out of the cooler, and it had to be doing at least fifty mph.

Everyone scattered.

Women were screaming. Babies were crying.

Dad was on the front porch of my grandfather's house with a shotgun.

I had climbed the fig tree that was in my grandparents' side yard.

The gator had gone under the house.

Yes, this gator had gone under my grandparent's house.

After sitting guard for a couple of hours, hoping the gator would emerge, my Dad and uncle took the two remaining gators back to the lake and released them.

But the third gator?

We never saw him again.

For the first couple of weeks when you left my grandparent's house, you'd always double-check the yard and the steps.

This story was always a classic in our family.

But it also taught me a lesson.

Be aware of the next step.

If someone had thought about what to do after the gator was in the cooler, then no one would have to be afraid to step off the porch.

This is so true for leaders.

> The stakes are high.
> Your decisions matter.
> You can't just throw caution to the wind
> and hope everything works out.
> You must look at your decision and then
> consider possible outcomes and responses
> to those scenarios.

Leaders can't afford for a gator to get loose and live under the house.

Your team will live in fear and worry if the future is secure.

Be like Dad...be brave enough to handle the most dangerous of situations but have people around you who will help you consider the next steps.

And for the record, I don't recommend alligator handling as a profession.

20. THROW A PARTY

I've always struggled in math.

Numbers and I are not a good combo.

In the sixth-grade, I found myself in remedial math. In other words, I wasn't progressing like the other students.

You were defined as "remedial" by the workbook you were able to work through.

I was in the yellow workbook, whereas 90% of the rest of the class seemed to work their way effortlessly through the green workbook.

Here I was, a full three workbooks behind the class -- Me and about three other characters who couldn't figure out that if a train left Philadelphia at 12:19 p.m. traveling at 518 mph and passed a car doing 65 mph going West, then how many apples did little Johnny have? (I hated those questions.)

I worked hard -- very hard.

Mr. Gilbeaux, my sixth-grade teacher, came to me and said, "Congratulations, Brian! You've advanced to the green workbook. You're just one workbook away from being with the rest of the class."

I couldn't wait to tell Dad.

For some reason, Dad picked me up from school that day.

"Dad, guess who got promoted from the yellow math workbook to the green math workbook?"

He paused for a moment and replied, "I bet it was that Chambers boy."

Full of joy and pride, I exclaimed, "It was me!!"

Dad celebrated me. He bragged on me. He went by the store and got us a Fanta Red soda and a honey bun. (That was a big deal in our house.)

Leaders celebrate others.

Let the team bring you the news.

Give them the opportunity to tell you, and then throw the party.

People need to know you're proud of them, not just in a generic sense but also in a specific one.

Tell them why you're celebrating!

Throw a party because of what was accomplished and pause to recognize the person's gifts and skills. After all, that's really what did everything. It's the person's learning and skills that you are celebrating.

Be like Dad...throw a party--even if it's an impromptu celebration with a bottle of Big Red soda and a honey bun snack cake.

21. SEE THE STARTING POINT

I called her mamaw.

She was my Dad's mom.

> Plump. Kind. Woman of faith. Loved to
> laugh. Glorious cook.

Her health began to fail the last few years of her
life, the result of diabetes and several strokes.

She lost the use of one side of her body. Her arm
and hand were unable to do anything.

My grandfather was unable to provide 24-hour
care at home, so she was admitted to a nursing
home in Winnfield, Louisiana.

Her diabetes progressed to where her legs had to
be amputated.

Anytime we visited, we would spend significant
chunks of time with her.

Stories would fill the air.

Laughter would erupt.

Mamaw would either be in a bed or sitting in a wheelchair.

Being in that place and in that condition wore on her soul.

Then a critical moment came for her and my Dad.

My grandmother asked my Dad if she could leave the nursing home and either go home and live with my grandfather or with us.

My Dad knew this was impossible with all of her health conditions and the round the clock care she would require, but Dad was still a son and loved his mom.

He didn't want to tell her "No" without context.

Dad told me he did the hardest thing he ever had to do.

He looked at her and said, "Mother, if you can go up and down the hallway of the nursing home in your wheelchair, we'll talk."

My grandmother put her hands on the wheels of the chair and pushed.

What happened?

She went in circle after circle.

She cried.

My Dad cried.

It was at that moment that my grandmother realized she was in the best hands at the nursing home.

Why did Dad do that?

My grandmother had to face her condition.

She had to be convinced by her own accord, not the opinion of someone else.

So, what my Dad did in making her face reality was kind and loving. Allowing her to live in a dream would have continued to generate false hope and unmet expectations.

After embracing her condition, Dad and my grandfather helped plan visits home and helped her see how life could be lived well in the nursing home.

That's leadership.

Was it hard?

Yes.

It took all the fortitude my Dad could muster.

But was it the right thing to do? Yes. Yes, it was.

Leaders must operate from a place of reality and not from false hope.

Clarity provides a way forward.

It puts everyone on the same page and allows the best future to come forth.

Be like Dad…help your team see reality and paint a future from that starting point.

22. YOU WON'T ALWAYS
BE HERE

It was one of the first things I saw when I walked through the front door.

The list was sitting on the kitchen counter near the telephone.

There were three columns, each with a distinct purpose.

I saw a name, phone number, and then a task/purpose.

The list was handwritten by my Dad.

When Dad learned that his cancer was terminal, he began preparing my mom for a future that didn't include him.

This was the purpose of the list.

"If the air conditioner breaks, call..."

"For help with retirement funds, call…"

"Regarding firewood, call...."

The list went on and on.

I was absolutely stunned.

My Dad had been diagnosed with stage 4 melanoma cancer, and rather than curling up in a ball and doing nothing, he planned.

His goal was to make Mom's future as comfortable and seamless as possible.

That's grit and fortitude.

Dad was looking past his death and what Mom would need once he was gone.

Let me be honest, Dad was stronger than I'll ever be.

I don't know where he found this kind of strength and determination.

But I respect it so much.

My selfishness is so deep that if you told me I had Stage IV cancer, I fear I'd be consumed with loathing and bitterness.

But not Dad.

He planned.
He knew life had to go on even if he didn't.

Leaders plan.

They see a world where they are not, but their influence remains.

Plan for that day.
Leave plans and instructions.
Help the next generation by showing
the way.

Be like Dad...realize you won't always be here, so do what you can to ease the burden of those who remain.

23. BE A PERSON OF
YOUR WORD

Getting Dad to talk about his time in Vietnam
often proved difficult.

I'd find various ways to ask questions, and he'd
always avoid them by changing the topic.

One afternoon we were on the river fishing.

I finally said, "Dad, I just have to know. Tell me
about Vietnam. What did you do?"

He turned the chair in the front of the boat and
faced me with a rod and reel in his hand, and said,

"Imagine being in an airplane over a war
zone. You can hear bullets hitting the side
of your plane. The pilot is trying to stay
high enough to avoid enemy fire. But my
job? The job of the plane I was on? We'd be
alerted that another plane was shot down.
We'd find the nearest landing area, go in,
land the plane, get out, strip as much
electrical equipment as possible out of the

crashed plane and then carry it back to our plane. The pilot would take off, sometimes under gunfire, and while we're in the air, me and my crew would try to fix the electronics of the plane that had been shot down. I've heard bullets hit the side of a plane. I've heard bombs explode. I've felt the sound of bombs going off against my chest."

I'm sure my eyes were bulging.

I replied, "Wow. I mean…wow. Anything else?"

Dad quipped, "There's a lot more. But we won't talk about it."

And with that, he went back to fishing.

I was left with so many questions.

> Was he scared?
> Did he want to quit?
> How did he control his fears?

I then asked, "Were you afraid? Did you want to quit?"

Dad bluntly proclaimed, "It was my job. I had given my word."

There it was.

Dad was a man of his word.

He did the job and did it to the best of his ability.

He knew that others depended on him.

His example set the tone for others on the plane.

If Jack was afraid, then everyone else would be afraid.

The lessons from this story are many for me as a leader. The one that stands out to me is…

…to be a person of your word.

Dad committed to doing a job, and he did it to the best of his ability, even when bullets riddled the side of his airplane.

Dad's integrity didn't depend on the severity of the situation.

His word was his bond, and nothing broke it.

Leaders, you can't quit, even if the going gets overwhelming.

You can't quit.

Your daily presence sets the tone and spreads belief and hope.

When the bullets start to fly, stand tall.

That's when your team needs you the most.

Don't flinch in the fight.

Be like Dad…be a person of your word.

24. HAVE A FEW CLOSE FRIENDS

Dad was the typical American guy.

By that, I mean he knew a lot of people but didn't have a lot of close friends.

I asked him one day about his friends and his lack thereof.

His response was shockingly honest.

> "Son, there are people in this world you can trust and people you can't. So far, I've learned there are a few I can trust, and when I meet some more who are trustworthy, you'll see that circle expand."

I'll give Dad this -- he didn't mince words.

> But Dad did have friends.

Sammy Thomas was probably his best friend, who was more like a brother.

They texted each morning about the weather and the latest news.

Robert Bamburg was a friend, and he and Dad would fish, tell stories, and work on projects together.

K.C. Collingsworth was another of Dad's buddies. They'd golf, fish, and swap stories.

These are the men that my Dad shared life with.

**Life is too long and tough
to go through it without some friends.**

These men and my Dad would go to the river or the golf course and laugh, harass each other like guys do, and tell some tall tales.

Get some people like that in your life.

It doesn't have to be a dozen people.

As a matter of fact, keep the circle small and tight of those you trust with your heart.

That's what Dad did.

We all need these kind of people in our lives.

**Leaders need people we can laugh with
and blow off steam with.**

Leaders have to be constantly "on stage" and need some friends who give them the opportunity to drop their guard and just relax.

For my Dad, Sammy, Robert, and K.C. were people he could trust.

He didn't have to worry about what was said when he was with them.

Life is tough, and it'll beat you up along the way.

Get yourself some friends who'll bring laughter, jokes, and perspective into your days.

You'll be a better person and leader because of it.

Be like Dad...have a few close friends you can trust.

25. BE GOOD AT SOMETHING

Dad loved baseball.

In high school, he was the starting pitcher for Calvin High School in Winn Parish.

He was good -- very good.

So much so that scouts came out to watch Dad.

He knew how to grip a baseball, so it curved just so over home plate.

Sliders and sinkers were part of his vocabulary.

He was all about some "high heat," which is what fastballs are called when thrown at the height of the batter's chest.

Dad's catcher was a man I came to call "Uncle Eddie."

Eddie Franks was a cousin of my Dad, and they were the same age. Being from the south, that meant he was called "Uncle."

Fast forward to when Eddie's son, Reggie, was in high school and was the pitcher.

One Saturday morning, there's a knock on the door, and there stands Uncle Eddie and Reggie. They wanted lessons from Dad.

We all bounded out to the front yard. For the next four hours, I listened and watched as my Dad explained the importance of a grip, how to release, and why you must focus on the target.

Within those few hours, Reggie knew how to throw a curve, slider, breaker, and fastballs.

Reggie grew frustrated about ninety minutes in, and his dad said, "Son, listen to the man. He knows what he's talking about."

That was a moment of pride for me.

Someone else recognized my Dad as an expert. That does something for a son's heart.

The lesson out of all this?

Be known for something.

Be so good at it that others will come to seek your help to get better at it.

No one goes and asks advice from a person who is just mediocre — they go to the best.

Be like Dad…be good at something and help others be good at it.

Dad 1952-53   Dad 1957-58

Grandma Sanders, Dad, Grandpa Sanders

Aunt Laverne (Dad's Sister), Dad, and their dog
1946-47

Mom and Dad at their wedding

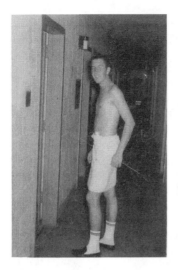

Dad in the Air Force
1962

Dad in the Air Force

Dad in Hawaii

Dad doing what he loved...fishing

Dad and Kayla (his Baby Girl)

Mom and Dad at our wedding

Me, Dad, Kayla, and Mom

Me and Dad

My favorite picture of Mom and Dad

26. EMBRACE THE TRUTH

The voice on the other end of the phone screamed...

"B!! AM I GOING TO DIE?!"

The phone rang at 11:30 p.m.

I had just drifted to sleep after a long day of travel.

He was screaming,

"DOES GOD CARE?"
"IS HE GOING TO LET ME DIE? I HAVE KIDS!"

I listened...

I just listened.

After he asked his questions and got his stuff out on the table, I finally said --

"Let me give you three truths.
(These three truths come from Jerry Bridges
book, *Trusting God*.)

First, God is sovereign. What you're going
through is not surprising God. For some
purpose beyond our understanding, He has
allowed this season of suffering to enter
your life."

I could hear his wife in the background, crying
while she also spoke comforting words to him.

"Second, God is wise. He doesn't just do
things willy-nilly. Purpose and planning are
behind His actions. We may not understand
His actions, but He's always at work and
moving wisely. He isn't making up the plan
as He goes along. He isn't scrambling,
hoping history works itself out. He has a
plan, and He's bringing it to pass.

Finally, God is loving. He loves you. He
cares deeply. With that being said, that
doesn't mean God doesn't allow pain in our
lives.

Remember this: the biggest problem you
ever had has been solved. Your sin is gone.
Jesus has forgiven you. You will not face
condemnation. He loves you. He loves your
wife and children. No matter what
happens, He loves you.

Keep these three truths in mind. Breathe deeply. Rest in Jesus. They don't answer all your questions...but they'll help you sleep."

Who was on the phone?

Mrs. Kayla and I never had kids of our own. The issue was with me. However, we've mentored kids through seminary and college for a number of years, so we have a ton of "kids."

On the phone was Steve Pupillo, one of our boys.

Steve was twenty-nine when the doctors told him he had tumors in his brain, legs, and one in his lung. His world fell apart.

Where was I when I took this call?

I was standing at the foot of my Dad's hospital bed in Shreveport, Louisiana.

You see, my Dad was fighting cancer and would lose that battle about ninety minutes after I got off the phone with Steve.

Yes, the last thing my Dad heard was me giving a mini-sermon to one of our "sons," -- one where I told him that God is sovereign, wise, and loving.

That gives me chill bumps.

Dad is in Heaven and is completely healed. That tells me God is sovereign, wise, and loving.

How is Steve?

He's cancer-free.

He's back to practicing medicine. That tells me God is sovereign, wise, and loving.

His wife Sarah and two children are all great.

Why did God allow Steve to get cancer?

I don't know all the reasons…but I do know one reason… it's so I could take a phone call at 11:30 p.m., and my Dad could hear about God's sovereignty, wisdom, and love. That's the grace and mercy of the Lord Jesus.

If while reading this you're struggling and doubting…remember…He is sovereign…He is wise…He is loving.

To Steve…love ya, young man. Proud of you.

To Dad…love and miss ya, Pops.

And to you, dear reader…

Be like Dad…before you leave this world, embrace the truth that God is sovereign, wise, and loving.

27. DEFEND THOSE
YOU LOVE

We were fishing.

For some reason, that's where most of our important conversations took place.

On this day, we discussed what color of fishing bait would result in a full cooler of fish.

I had just asked Kayla to marry me -- and she said yes.

The date was set, and plans were in full motion.

My Dad never had a daughter.

He LOVED Kayla. She was his "Baby Girl."

If we were home for Christmas and she wanted a fire in the fireplace…there was a fire. It didn't matter if it was seventy-five degrees. There was a fire in that fireplace.

Here we were on the river, just Dad and me throwing baits out in the water and chewin' the fat about work and life.

All of a sudden…out of nowhere, he interrupts the conversation, turns around, and locks eyes with me.

He said,

> "Boy, you ever hurt Kayla…I'll whip the hell out of you."

I replied, "Yes, sir. Understood."

With that, he went back to fishing and telling tall tales.

He never brought that up again.

> For the record, I've never knowingly hurt Kayla.

If Dad loved you, he protected you, and he let those around you know it.

Kayla was the daughter he never had, and he adored her.

Leaders need to protect their teams.
Stand up for your team.

When people from the outside hurl accusations or bring a complaint, listen and be empathetic but have the backs of your team members. Your team will be more dedicated to the mission and vision.

> Put your team first.
> Take care of them.
> Defend them.

Be in their corner.

I wouldn't recommend telling a disgruntled vendor that you'll "whip the hell out of them," but you get the point.

Be like Dad...defend those you love and care about.

28. OWN YOUR MISTAKES

It was an odd season in Dad's life.

He was out of high school and waiting to be shipped to basic training for the Air Force.

At the time, Dad was living with his parents.

Being from the south, our family has true southern names.

Such is the case with Uncle Willie and Aunt Marcella.

Uncle Willie was the brother of Dad's Mom.

If there's one thing my Dad enjoyed doing as a young man, it was going to a dance.

Oh…if there's one thing Uncle Willie and Aunt Marcella liked to do as a young couple, it was dancing.

It was a Friday night, and Dad was getting ready to go out.

My grandfather said to Dad, "Son, now don't go over to that Lake Club. Stuff has happened over there. Me and your momma worry about you when you go."

Dad promised he wouldn't. Out the door, he dashed.

But Dad lied.

He went to the Lake Club.

To his surprise, there was Uncle Willie and Aunt Marcella.

They all danced, laughed, and had a good Louisiana Friday night.

Saturday morning came, and Dad crawled out of bed.

Sitting at the kitchen table drinking coffee, my grandfather says to Dad, "Your Uncle Willie called."

Dad, who is half awake, grunts a "Huh?"

My grandfather, with the precision of a surgeon wielding a knife, says, "Yep. He just wanted to make sure you got home safely from the Lake Club."

Dad knew He was busted.

Dad loved this story. He told it often.

For me, as a leader, it contains several key principles.

First, always tell the truth.

Never try to hide what can be easily known.

Dad was young and figured telling my grandfather what he wanted to hear was easier than simply telling the truth.

That will always come back to bite a leader.

Deviating from the truth will never end well and will cost you credibility.

As a leader, the two greatest things you possess are credibility and trust.

Don't burn either of those because you want to take a shortcut and think you're above telling the truth.

Second, leaders call people on their crap.

My grandfather didn't just sweep the situation under the rug. In a creative way, he let my Dad know that he knew.

Leaders don't ignore situations; we confront them.

Whether it be a lie we uncover or a task that has gone undone, leaders handle stuff.

To ignore the situation is to surrender the chair of leadership.

Finally, don't be ashamed to share your stories.

Dad lied. But he shared the story anyway.

Why would he do that?

He knew he was flawed, and everyone could relate to it.

Also, he was teaching me a lesson not to hide stuff from him.

A conversation beforehand is much easier than a confrontation resulting from a lie or hiding information.

Be like Dad...when you mess up, own it and tell the story so others can learn from your mistakes.

29. DON'T GIVE UP

> "Mr. Sanders, how have you been working for the last five years? Most men would have crumbled under the pain. How have you done this?"

Those were the words from Dad's first visit to an arthritis specialist.

Dad responded with,

> "I just kept going. I had to keep going for my family, my job, my responsibilities. I couldn't let any of those people or things down. You just set your mind to ignore the pain and accomplish what is in front of you."

I've never forgotten those words.

You need to understand, Dad's hands and feet had been giving him great pain.

He didn't complain about it.

Oh, he'd mention it, but if you tried to offer him any sympathy, he would instantly react and reject any offer.

Dad was not a delicate flower.

Words I would use to describe him: Tough. Rugged. Strong. Stubborn.

Dad endured.

I never remember him taking a sick day.

Even though he had crippling arthritis, he went to the paper mill every single day. He led the electrical team, climbing stairs and walking the massive operation, ensuring all systems worked properly.

**Leaders don't get to choose the hand they're dealt,
but you do choose if you'll march through it.**

Dad chose to push on and never complained.

Even with his arthritis, he worked, hunted, and fished. He still took Mom on dates.

Leaders keep going.

No matter how strong the headwinds, you keep making progress.

You can't pause and complain.

Doing so doesn't help achieve the goal.

It poisons the soul.

No matter what you're facing, keep your eyes on the horizon.

The goal can still be achieved.

Be like Dad... don't give up.

30. HAVE A ROUTINE

Dad had a routine.

The first task of his day?

...a few cups of coffee and the weather.

Coffee because he was addicted to it, and the weather since his ability to go fishing was directly tied to the winds and rain.

He'd then text his best friend, and they would discuss the weather.

There was a fisherman's flip calendar next to Dad's chair.

Each day held a proverb or a funny quip about fishing, but if you looked closely, you'd see writing on some of the pages.

If Dad had a particularly good day at fishing, he'd write it on that calendar.

Perhaps he had bagged a six-point deer -- it would be on that calendar.

Part of his routine was to see what had been done in the past and let it help him make decisions about today.

Routines are good.

> They give us stability, direction, and benchmarks.
> The right routine generates long-term progress.

Dad could look at his daily flip calendar and see when he caught the most fish or when the deer were most active. Time and record-keeping gave him that ability.

As a leader,

> Invest in your people by coaching and encouraging them.
> Take time each week to pour into them some leadership truth.
> Walk with them through a great book. Give them scenarios and ask them to react as a leader.

That routine will produce great benefits. You won't see it in a week or two. But in a year or two, it will produce amazing dividends.

> People will grow.

Some will identify as a leader, while others
reveal themselves as not having the gift.

Get in the routine of tracking numbers and
results.

Share those results.
Allow the team to see trends. They'll make
better choices because of it.

For you, personally?

Invest in yourself.
Get in the routine of reading and listening.
Better yourself as a leader.

Results won't be immediate, but you'll look back
in a year and see how you've grown.

You'll make better decisions.

Be like Dad...have a routine that makes you better
at what you love to do.

31. EMBRACE NEW IDEAS AND METHODS

Dad decided that they'd take the plunge.

It was time to discard the flip phones and get an iPhone.

We ended up at the Verizon store. At the time, they were giving away an iPhone 5s for free.

Dad was always a man looking for a good deal, so he jumped on that.

He was never much for technology — email was about the extent of his computer use.

He'd grumble about people who always had their face in an iPhone and how they'd tap away at a little screen. He'd exclaim, "Why don't they just call? It would be faster!"

But then, Dad and Mom got their iPhones.

He was like a duck to water.

The phone hadn't been in his hand for fifteen minutes, and he was texting people.

I stood in amazement as I watched my Dad text.

He quipped, "This is pretty nifty. You can tell people stuff without having to call them and have some long-drawn-out needless conversation."

He'd tap on the Safari icon and search for any piece of information he wanted.

Apple Maps was his favorite. Even if he knew where he was going, he'd fire up that app and let it guide him to his destination.

The next day, Dad and Kayla were going to town, and he decided to drive.

While driving, Dad reaches down and picks up his iPhone, and begins to text someone.

Kayla said, "Poppa, I love you — but you're going to get us killed if you text and drive. You fuss at us kids for texting and driving; now it's time for you to do the same."

He responded with, "You're right, baby girl. You're right."

With that, he put the phone down.

Dad would never call you. He'd FaceTime and my, how he loved to do that.

The phone would ring, and you might see a video of a fish he had caught, a deer he had killed, or his face because he simply wanted to chat.

Dad taught me that people are never too old to learn.

We can adapt and learn new things.

As a leader, you never reach your capacity to learn or change.

You can get better. You can improve.

Stop thinking you're done or that you've reached your limit.

You haven't.

If there's breath in your body, then you can begin a new journey and better yourself to attain it.

You are who you make yourself.

Perhaps a particular idea didn't work.

Try another way.

You can adapt to new technology.

There are new ideas you can explore.

Criticism doesn't have to destroy your motivation.

You're not stupid.

**Failure is a lesson learned,
not a cage for your identity to live in.**

Be like Dad…embrace new ideas and methods.

32. BE CRYSTAL CLEAR

There's a famous story in my family, and Dad loves to tell it each Christmas when the family gathers.

I couldn't have been more than seven or eight years old.

Somehow I got in a fight with some other boys. (There's a shock.) One of the boy's moms saw this and began yelling at us. I responded to her, "Lady, my Dad will whip you. He takes care of the big ones!"

The lady went into her house and laughed. And I think she was friends with my parents and called and told them about my bold proclamation.

I came home and told Dad what had happened. Through laughter, he said, "Yes, son, I'll always be there to fight the big ones."

A year or two later, we were visiting my grandparents, Dad's parents, and I was giving my grandmother some serious grief.

She quipped, "Little man, I'll get a switch and wear you out."

It was then I said, "Oh no, you won't. My Dad said he'd take care of the big ones, and that includes you!"

She sat down and began to laugh. I was a little fella, but I still remember her laughing.

"Little Mister," she said in between laughs, "I handled your Daddy, and I'll handle you."

She didn't whip me.

> She was laughing too hard to use that switch.

It was a few hours later that Dad came to me.

> "Son, we need to talk about who the big ones are and who they aren't."

After that little conversation, it was crystal clear that my grandmother was no longer on that list.

Words will sometimes require clarifying.

As a little boy, I took Dad literally. Anyone bigger or taller than me was his problem.

Your team or congregation will need you to offer clarifying statements.

When communicating important concepts, explain them as though everyone knows nothing.

Ask for feedback. Refine the message. Make sure everyone is on the same page and has the same understanding.

Yes, it will take extra time, but you'll soon see how beneficial doing so was.

Be like Dad...be willing to explain until things are crystal clear.

33. LAUGH AT YOURSELF

"Look at me. I have the figure of an eighteen-year-old -- a very out of shape eighteen-year-old."

"I'm so pretty that women just swoon around me. They usually swoon from running away from me."

Dad was good at self-deprecating humor.

It put others at ease.

Dad's personality was larger than life.

His skills on the river, in the woods, and on the golf course were well known.

His integrity was as solid as an oak tree.

Dad was not perfect — he was deeply flawed like any of us, but he was also great. His character and strength entered the room before his body did.

I don't know how Dad learned to do it, but he did it well.

His humor in making fun of himself won him friends from all around.

It made him likable and, most importantly, approachable.

Be approachable.
Be likable.

If you're neither, your leadership will have a short shelf life.

Use the trick that my Dad and other leaders have used -- make fun of yourself.

It drops the other person's guard and lets them know you're human, just like them.

> Surrender your pride for the good of the team.

The ability to laugh at yourself reveals the strength of character.

Your team needs to know that you can handle the jokes of yourself and others and whatever storm may come to your path.

Being humble enough to laugh at yourself builds both relationships and trust.

Be like Dad...have the ability to laugh at yourself.

34. BE YOURSELF

Believer.

Doubter.

Struggler.

Non-church goer.

Despiser of fake people.

User of four-letter words

Critic of the Federal Government.

Watcher of every movie about Jesus.

Not a big reader of the Book about Him.

Lover of people.

Short-tempered.

Storyteller.

Loud laugher.

Simultaneously generous and selfish.

Loved my Mom with an unmatched love.

Faithful.

Fierce friend.

Defender of his family.

Impatient and easily aggravated.

All those things were true of my Dad.

As I've written this little book about him, I want to make sure you understand that Dad wasn't perfect.

**Perfection isn't necessary
to have an impact on someone's life.**

**You can still provide a foundation
for someone to accomplish much.**

Even with all his foibles and flaws, Dad's influence helped me be the leader I am today.

His example built a foundation for me to keep going even in the face of great resistance.

Still, there's a bigger principle at play.

Dad wasn't perfect, but he was great.

And there's the lesson.

I don't have to be perfect to impact others.

All leaders should release themselves from that expectation.

Great leadership isn't defined by flawlessness.

It's the ability to recover from the flaws and to adjust sails when the winds change.

Every leader has a history of mistakes.

>Lean on those.
>Learn from them.

Be reminded that you've survived every stumble to this point, and you'll bounce back from the next one.

>Don't try and be perfect.

You'll only make yourself and those around you miserable.

>Know who you are -- flaws and all.

Your team knows your shortcomings. Don't hide them.

It will inspire them to keep trying when they have a leader who fights back after being down.

>Own your misfires.
>Work at being better.
>Drop perfectionism.

Be like Dad…be yourself, own your flaws, and impact others.

35. USE CARING CANDOR

The little church was down a single lane road.

Trees lined either side with the limbs hanging over.

The road finally opened up to a gravel parking lot facing Hickory Grove Baptist Church.

It was a Sunday night, and the occasion was my first sermon.

Mom and Dad were there.

My topic was, "Who Wrote the Bible?"

I had to be a freshman or sophomore in high school, and I was eager to show that I was no fool.

During my sermon at the small country church, I began name-dropping.

Shakespeare.
Thomas Aquinas.

Dante'.
Lord Byron.
Mark Twain.

The names just kept pouring out.

I made the point that God was the Master Author.

But I made it at the expense of my audience.

Mom and Dad both hugged me and told me they were proud.

Later that week, Dad and I were in his bass boat fishing.

"Son, your sermon was excellent." That's how Dad opened the conversation.

"What I'm about to say doesn't take away any of the pride I have for you," he said with great care.

Then he said, "Know your audience. Who will you be speaking to? Based on that, choose your words."

"I think I get it. I overdid it with Shakespeare, Byron, and Twain, didn't I?"

Through a laugh, he said, "Just a little. When people leave, you want them to remember what you said, not go scrambling for a dictionary."

Be understandable.

Having the right pitch and cadence doesn't matter if people don't understand the content.

Great communicators
make the complicated understandable.

Often, the great intellectual can make the easiest of concepts complicated.

Make it simple —
use stories that the audience will understand.

Since that day, I've always considered my audience.

His conversation made me a better speaker.

His voice and that lesson still resonate today.

To be a better leader,
one must be understood.

Consider your audience.
Plan your words accordingly.

Because he took the time to address the issue, Dad made me a better communicator.

Be like Dad…use caring candor to help others improve.

36. TRY SOMETHING NEW

Dad wasn't much for new kinds of food.

Before I was born, Mom and Dad were invited by some friends to play cards and have dinner.

On the menu was lasagna.

Dad had never eaten it.

NEVER.

Mom kept trying to tell him that it was pasta with meat and cheese, and he'd like it.

Nope. Dad would not hear it.

That evening, before leaving for their friend's house, Dad ate three bologna sandwiches.

He wanted to be full, so when the lasagna came around, he could honestly say he wasn't hungry.

Mom and Dad arrive, and they're seated at the table.

Their friend puts a massive pan of lasagna in the center of the table.

Dad takes the tiniest of helpings.

He said that when he tasted it, he's pretty sure he heard angels sing.

What did Dad do?

Let me quote my Mom,

"He ate half the pan. Literally…he ate half the pan."

This story always makes me laugh.

It is quintessential, Dad.

Something he swore he'd hate became something he enjoyed.

There's your leadership lesson.

Plan ahead.

If you must —

plan for the worst.

You may even have to eat three bologna sandwiches.

But once you're in the middle of the situation —

**pause and see if what you've been dreading
is as bad as you thought it would be.**

Perhaps, like Dad, you'll be a fan of whatever it is
that landed in front of you.

Leaders adapt to their circumstances.

Embrace change.
Celebrate it.
Allow others to see you enjoying it.
It'll help them embrace it as well.

Be like Dad…try something new.

37. ENJOY THE SUNSHINE
AFTER STORMS

The baseball uniforms were orange and white.

I was part of a team called The Twins.

Coach Chambers was leading us through a regular season.

When you're in sixth-grade, being part of a winning sports team is a big hairy deal.

Our game was on a baseball diamond in Alexandria, Louisiana.

The game was close.

It was my time to bat.

As I came into the dugout from my position in the right field, I didn't notice the lip of the dugout floor.

The floor, made of wood, was about two inches higher than the ground.

There was a bench in the dugout made of metal with sharp edges.

Mom and Dad were in the stands for this game.

Parents were cheering.

Umpires were scolding players for all the smack talk.

As I made my way to the dugout to grab a bat and a helmet, my foot caught that two-inch lip of the floor.

It sent me falling headfirst toward the corner of the bench.

The sharp metal corner of the bench caught just above my right eye.

I hit the floor with a massive thud.

Blood was everywhere.

Dad saw me fall and was climbing out of the stands before I ever hit the ground.

Mom was right on his heels.

The force of the impact knocked me out.

I woke up in the emergency room, surrounded by doctors who were sewing several stitches.

Mom and Dad were by my bed.

Mom was relieved that I was okay.

Dad said, "Son, you have some guests here to see you."

He stepped back, and the entire Twins team poured into the tiny room at the hospital.

They had won the game and dedicated the win to me.

I'll never forget being surrounded by the guys and them telling me the story of how they won the game.

During all that, I made eye contact with Dad, and he just winked at me.

He knew this was a moment that a boy needed to enjoy, and he let me relish in it.

On the way home, I commented how great it was that we won the game and how the guys had dedicated the win to me.

Dad commented, "Ya see, son, good things do result out of painful stuff."

I've never forgotten that lesson.

Never.

The game would have never been dedicated to me if I had not busted my head open.

As some say, I would have never known the joy of a mountaintop if I had not experienced the low of the valley.

Some of the lowest points of your life

will result in unimaginable pain.

**But they'll teach you lessons
and reveal strength you didn't know you had.**

Don't waste those experiences.

Be like Dad...enjoy the sunshine after a storm.

38. ASK HARD QUESTIONS

He didn't care much for myths or fairy tales.

Dad's world was always based in reality.

If you were watching a TV show about Bigfoot or UFO's, he'd raise an eyebrow and ask,

"Are you kidding me with this? With all the cell phones, cameras, satellites, and trail cams...if there was something out there... don't you think we would have found it? Also, with as many people in the world who have guns... there's a good chance we would have killed whatever unknown critter might be running around."

While that's funny, it's also true.

One of Dad's life truths was to be anchored in reality.

When Dad was discovered to have lymphoma cancer in his lungs, liver, and hips -- one of the first questions he asked the doctor was how long he would live.

The doc skirted the issue.

Dad said, "Give it to me straight. How long do I have? A year? Do I have a year?"

The doctor said, "I'd say a year is a good number."

Dad replied, "Let's be clear. I'd like to avoid as much pain as possible."

Reality gives you a path forward.
It allows you to make better decisions.

For Dad, he made decisions about his end of life care -- like whether he wanted to be cremated or buried.

Living in a dreamland wouldn't have served him, Mom, or any of the family well.

Reality works.

You need a plan for the future, but to get to that future, you must begin from where you are.

Start with reality.

If you don't know where you are, then you'll never get to where you need to be.

Slow down.

Assess where you are.
Be brutally honest about your situation.

Only then can you plan the next steps.

Be like Dad...ask hard questions to have an accurate view of what you're facing.

39. BE COURAGEOUS

Dad spent twenty years in the Air Force.

He was stationed at bases in Hawaii, California, South Dakota, Indiana, Nebraska, Washington DC, and Louisiana.

When people ask me where I'm from, I often reply with,

> "Throw a dart at a map. I've probably lived there."

Dad loved the Air Force.

He also loved the stories of its leaders.

He loved to tell the story of General Curtis LeMay of the US Air Force.

> LeMay loved cigars.

There would always be one lit hanging from his mouth.

One day, the plane LeMay was to fly was being fueled.

>Fumes were everywhere.
>The smell of fuel filled the fuselage of the plane.

And there's Lemay with a cigar.

A sergeant approached Lemay and told the general that the cigar could light the fumes and cause the plane to explode.

Lemay famously quipped, "Son, it wouldn't dare."

Dad told me that story no less than a hundred times, and each time he'd roar with laughter.

>He'd also use the story to drive home a point.

More often than not, the point he was trying to get across to me is that I was to own the moment.

When others are gripped with fear and don't believe, I need to believe, and others will see me as strong.

Someone needs to dare the situation to blow up and not fear the outcome.

That's a powerful leadership principle.

When the team is full of fear, you must be confident.

Sales are down, but you must believe they can rebound and inspire the team to close the deals.

The economy takes a dip and sends fear through everyone -- you must stand strong and share a vision that will allow the organization to sail through the storm.

A key leader resigns, and it creates doubt that certain goals can be accomplished -- your job is to replace that leader and motivate that team to achieve those goals.

Be like Dad...when others tremble, courageously stand.

40. POINT TO THE TRUTH

I had been at a revival service -- a very long, tiring, and guilt-driven revival service.

At the time, I was in high school and worked at a radio station that played country music.

After class, I'd drive to the station and do the afternoon-drive shift. On Saturdays I worked from 6 a.m.-- 1 p.m.

A traveling evangelist family hosted this revival service.

> I see now that their goal wasn't long-lasting life change, but rather how many people they could get to the altar.

The evangelist screamed into the handheld microphone,

> "There is something you must give up! If you're not at this altar confessing your sin

and possibly changing your career because it doesn't honor God, then you'll leave here tonight condemned!"

Well, that statement scared me.

So I went to the altar, afraid but couldn't think of anything I needed to confess.

Seventy-five percent of the church was already down there, kneeling and praying.

I join them.

The evangelist meets me with a bear hug and says, "What will you give up, brother? Do you need to quit your job?"

As an impressionable sixteen-year-old, I said, "Well, I'm in radio, and I play country music."

Sweet baby Moses.

You would have thought I had just confessed to a major crime.

He began to say,

> "You need to leave here tonight, repentant and ready to stop playing that music that celebrates the devil. Do you agree to do that? Say it now!!"

I said, "Yes, sir," and went back to my pew.

The next day I was riding with Dad to Shreveport, which is about an hour's drive.

I unfolded the whole conversation to him and asked him what he thought.

Dad had a strong response. A. VERY. STRONG. RESPONSE.

Now mind you, Dad didn't attend church, but he believed Jesus was real.

He said,

> "Son, the man manipulated you and
> everyone else who was there. He convinced
> you that radio was wrong; God didn't.
> Don't allow a man bent on controlling a
> crowd of people to get inside your head
> and make you leave a job that you love. I'm
> no church-goer, but I don't think that would
> make God happy."

Dad was right.

I didn't quit the radio station.

However, I did quit going to that revival and listening to that evangelist.

What neither Dad nor I knew was that he was teaching me the principle of Christian freedom.

He also laid the groundwork for me to distinguish between a person's voice and the voice of God.

And yes, they are two different things.

God will speak through people.

He does call us to repent, but not through individuals who want to manipulate and control a crowd.

I spent three years at that radio station playing country music.

Because I stayed, I was able to influence the management to allow me to play one Christian song per hour.

That would have never happened had I left due to the strong-arming of an overzealous evangelist.

Be wise to the lesson that Dad taught me.

**Learn to distinguish the voice of God
from the voice of a person.**

God wants you to be more like Jesus and live in His freedom.

A controlling and abusive evangelist wants to give you rules and live under guilt and condemnation.

Know the difference.

Be like Dad…point people to truth and away from manipulation.

41. ADORE YOUR SPOUSE

It was the 1960s, and there was a dance.

He went with his military buddies.

She was there with her friends.

This particular night was the first time he ever laid eyes on her.

He leaned over to his friend and said, "See that girl right there? I'm going to marry her."

And marry her he did.

Six weeks later, he was at an altar, and she walked down the aisle.

Yep, they were married six weeks after meeting at that dance.

That's how my Mom and Dad met and were married.

He adored my Mom.

Even after being married for fifty years, they would hold hands.

You could hear him telling Mom that she was beautiful. It was something he regularly did.

Certain music would come on, and they'd start dancing across the floor of the den at their house.

Did they ever have words?

Ummm…yes.

Just because they loved each other deeply didn't mean there was an absence of arguments.

Dad set an example of how a husband should love, honor, protect, and provide for his wife.

They both illustrated how love should endure both good and bad days.

He was always proud of Mom; he was never ashamed of her.

She was his confidante.

They leaned on each other during difficult times and celebrated during the good.

Those are lessons that went deep into my heart.

Whatever measure of husband I am, I owe it to my Dad.

He set the example.

And the bar he established is high....very high.

Want to be a better husband?

Be like Dad.

He was faithful, honest, kind, proud, and
adoring.

Do that, and your marriage could last over fifty
years...just like theirs.

Be like Dad...adore your spouse.

42. BE THE EXAMPLE

The boat was cruising along under the darkness of a late night.

Dad and his friend, Dave Massage, and I were fishing on Kincaid Lake in Alexandria, Louisiana.

A massive" thud" noise was followed by an abrupt stop. The motor was running, but there was no forward momentum.

The boat was not moving.

In the middle of the night, we were stuck in the middle of a lake.

Dad lowered the motor and tried to go forward…nothing.

He thought maybe we could reverse because the motor was running…the propeller was spinning, but no movement.

After figuring out that the motor was working, it then became apparent that we were lodged on a large stump.

The boat had perfectly "landed" itself on what was left of a tree trunk.

Due to the stump, we were sitting a bit higher than normal in the water.

Dad came to the center of the boat and began to rock it back and forth, trying to free us.

Then Dad and Dave were both rocking the boat.

Water began to lap into where we were sitting.

Dad pulled off his shirt and said,

> "Fellas, looks like I'm going in to push up and back on the boat to get us out of here."

Dave interrupted, "Jack...whoa...just stop. There are snakes and gators in that water. It's after 10 p.m., and we can't see anything..."

> "Well, either one of us goes in, or we stay out here all night," Dad exclaimed.

You really couldn't argue with Dad's reasoning, so the next thing you hear is a massive plunge.

Dad went to the front of the boat, and using the stump as leverage, he pushed us off, and the boat was free.

We got home around midnight with no fish, and Dad was cold and wet.

Some situations call for extreme solutions.

Was it ideal for Dad to get in the water?

Nope, but it was Dad's boat, not Dave's.

I offered to get in the lake, but Dad wouldn't let me.

He wanted to protect his son and not put me in harm's way.

In those moments, Dad was the epitome of a great leader.

> He did what was right for the team.
> He led by example.

Other options were exhausted before he got in the water.

The fact that we went home without fish didn't count as a loss.

This night was a win because everyone got home safely, and the boat was okay.

Sometimes getting your team through a storm is the win.

Being the example and showing them that there are times when a leader rolls up his sleeves and gets wet is the win.

Be like Dad…jump in and be the example for your team.

43. BE PATIENT

Time has a way of taking that which was aggravating and making it funny.

Dad was famous for frying fish.

It's a Louisiana delicacy, and no one did it better.

Yet, he'd be on the back patio with his fryer, and out of nowhere, he'd start to scream at the top of his lungs, "Ruth!! Ruth!! Ruth!!"

Mom would go running to the back door with an elevated heart rate, just waiting for news that something was wrong.

Swinging open the door, she'd say,

"Jack, you okay? What's wrong?"

Dad would respond with, "Could ya bring me some paper towels? I need some to set the fish on to soak up the grease."

It was then a conversation would begin about how to communicate.

> "Instead of screaming like the world is ending, just come to the door and ask for the paper towels."

We look back on this now and laugh.

Dad would do this to Mom, Kayla, me, and anyone else who might be at the house while he was cooking fish.

And what's funny...he never changed.

In marriage, work, and church life, we never lose the quirks that irritate others.

As you lead and work with others, you'll encounter things that touch every nerve in your body.

**Practice candor and
help people change what they can.**

While Dad's hollering may have startled us the first thousand times he did it, the second thousand we knew to grab some paper towels and walk outside.

There's a bigger lesson in all this.

To live this life with others,

you'll have to learn to practice grace.

No one is perfect -- not a single one of us.

As a result, show grace.

Be like Dad and those around him…change what you can and roll with the rest.

44. BE THE ANCHOR

Dad loved his riding lawnmower.

He'd kick that thing into fourth gear and start making the rounds to make his yard look great.

Following that, he'd trim around the bushes and trees.

Once or twice a year, he'd work on shaping plants and trees.

It was a summer day, and he'd been working in the yard.

> He was calm.
> Collected.
> His voice even with no excitement whatsoever.

He opens the door and says to Mom, "I'm going to the hospital. I'll be right back."

Mom hears the word hospital and immediately reacts, "Jack! What's wrong?"

Without any emotion, he says, "A baby snake bit me. I'm going to run uptown and be right back."

They haul off to the emergency room, where they give Dad a bit of anti-venom and some meds.

Another episode comes to mind when Dad had killed a deer.

He was skinning and cleaning it so he could have it butchered for the meat.

The knife he was using slipped and came across his thumb.

Not to be graphic, but it sliced off the top of his thumb.

He showed it to me while being completely calm.

He slipped off to the emergency room, where they bandaged it.

In situations where others could be prone to overreact, Dad would make sure he didn't.

Dad saw it as his role to be the unemotional one.

Why?

Because in those situations, emotions didn't help solve the problem. They had the potential to make it worse.

And there's the lesson...

know when to be calm.

You have to read the room and realize that everyone else could react, and as the leader, you can't.

The leader must project confidence and assurance,
so the rest of the team remains grounded in what is true
and not get lost in what could be.

Want to be a better leader?

Be like Dad...be the anchor when the sea is nothing but a storm.

45. MOTIVATE OTHERS TO
BE BETTER

It was the first brand-new vehicle I ever had.

As a matter of fact, it was the first car I had ever bought on my own.

I was out of college and in seminary and home for the weekend.

It was a 1991 or 1992 black Ford Ranger stick shift with a maroon interior.

Dad was with me at the dealership and asked, "Son, you can drive a stick shift. Right?"

Sure!

I exuded all the confidence in the world.

Truth be told, I had only driven a stick shift maybe once or twice in my life.

I figured I'd buy the truck and then learn.

Dad finally got the truth out of me and was not amused.

He drove the truck to his house and then left me to it.

I plopped in the driver's seat and put it in reverse, and stumbled out of the driveway.

Dad just walked into the house and shut the door.

I began driving the small two-seater truck all over their small town.

After driving for an hour and getting the basic hang of the stick shift, I stopped at the home of some friends.

Unknown to me, Dad was out driving and looking for me just to make sure I was safe.

He saw the truck parked at the home of my friends.

All I know is that the phone rang.

The call was for me.

It was Dad.

> "What are you doing visiting? You need to be out driving that truck. You live in a major city, New Orleans. Get your butt out of that house and drive that truck. Drive it until it becomes second nature."

All I remember is saying, "Yes, sir," and then driving that truck around their small town for hours and hours.

Dad was right.

I needed to get familiar with the truck before heading to the large city of New Orleans.

Thanks to Dad "motivating" my tail, I was able to navigate all the traffic and interstates of Crescent City.

Even though I was a grown man and could make my own decisions, Dad knew what was best and communicated it.

There are so many lessons from this story.

Be honest.

Honesty helps you adapt to new environments and technology and sometimes…new vehicles.

Be willing to listen.

I'm thankful I listened to Dad and drove that truck for hours and hours. It was easier to steer through New Orleans because I had.

Practice.
Get better at your craft.
Stop assuming you know everything.
Be open to learning.

Be like Dad…motivate others to be better.

46. STAND UP FOR WHAT
IS TRUE

I was sneaking books home and hiding them
under the bed.

Mom found them.

She and Dad confronted me.

Before you get the wrong idea, they weren't dirty
books, but they were books that concerned them.

They were books published by The Watchtower
Society.

Yes, I was reading and studying stuff given
to me by a Jehovah's Witness.

In case you're not familiar with them, The
Jehovah's Witnesses are a religious cult founded in
America in the early 1900s.

My high school counselor answered some of my spiritual questions and began giving me books to read.

Mom and Dad immediately took the books away from me.

Their next step was to meet with my high school counselor.

Yes, they met face to face with him, returned the books, and made it clear this topic was to never come up again.

I'll never forget watching Mom and Dad leave the high school.

For the record, my high school counselor NEVER brought up the topic again.

Even though Dad didn't attend church, he knew the truth.

He knew what was right and wrong when it came to basic orthodoxy.

Dad, along with Mom, protected me from a cult.

And there's the lesson…

protect your team — protect your family.

Stand for what is right.

Brace up, for there will be times when what needs to be said must be done so face-to-face.

Love your team enough that you'll protect them from coming danger, but take the time to tell them why you're taking those actions.

One more thing, Mom and Dad sat me down that evening and explained the consequences if I ever discussed those topics with my high school counselor ever again.

They loved me enough to put up a guardrail that kept me from being led astray.

Be like Dad (and Mom)...stand up for what is true.

47. SURROUND YOURSELF WITH THE BEST

Dad knew the things he couldn't do.

Perhaps it's better to say that he knew his skill set and stuck to that.

He didn't have the patience to build a storage shed.

The shortcuts he took would always leave it crooked.

No one ever asked Dad to fix their car.

He understood how a motor worked, but he didn't quite have the patience to troubleshoot each item.

Dad would tinker with things he didn't understand to figure them out.

However, at the end of the day, Dad knew his limits.

He wasn't afraid to call in people who knew more than he did.

Let me be clear -- Dad had a friend for every limitation that he had.

> In other words, he had formed a team of friends who were skilled in his weaknesses.

That example impacted me dramatically.

It screamed to me that I didn't have to know everything.

Rather, I should focus on my strengths and surround myself with those who excelled in my weaknesses.

Be that kind of leader.

Know your wheelhouse --

No one has skills that include EVERYTHING.

> Take an inventory as to your strengths and weaknesses.

> Build a team that can make you strong in areas where you are weak.

Be like Dad…surround yourself with people who excel at your shortcomings.

48. BE GENEROUS

I had graduated from college and was soon to leave for New Orleans to attend seminary.

Dad had to work the morning I was to depart.

It was early...very, very early.

He knocked on the bedroom door and woke me up, and then stepped into the room.

"Son, you got enough money for your trip to seminary and school?" he asked.

Still wiping sleep from my eyes, I replied, "Sir?"

He repeated the question, "Do you have enough money for the trip and classes?"

"I'm hoping to get a job at the campus radio station. I have enough to get me in school and dorm rent for the first semester. I should be okay." I answered.

He opened his wallet and counted out five crisp one hundred dollar bills.

"Here, take this. I'll tell ya Momma that I gave you this when I see her later," he explained.

"But, Dad. I have enough."

"Son, there aren't many things I can do for you anymore. Take the money."

I took the $500 and hugged his neck.

He kissed me on the cheek and said, "Love ya, boy. Proud of you. Be careful driving. Call us when you get there with your new phone number."

With that, he left the room as he wiped a tear.

I made it to the seminary, paid for classes and dorm rent. I opened a bank account and called my parents.

Dad wanted to make sure I was prepared.

He had done all he could do to equip me for the next phase of my life.

The last thing he could do was give me money to help with my semester of seminary, and he was proud to do it.

Prepare your teams.
Equip them to face the future.
When you think you've done all you can do,
do some more.

While you're taking them through books, blogs, and leadership videos, do something a little extra...give them a little cash every now then.

Why?

They need to see you being generous.

Jack Welch, the famed CEO of GE, teaches that every leader needs to have a generosity gene in their DNA.

Start practicing that generosity with your team.

They'll feel appreciated and learn to be generous leaders themselves.

Be like Dad...open your wallet and be generous.

49. EXCEED YOUR GOALS

It was a tiny blue house in Blacksburg, VA.

The rooms were oddly configured.

As strange as it was, it was home for Kayla and me.

After living and working in New Orleans for nearly fifteen years, I had accepted a job in Virginia to oversee multiple radio stations.

We had been in Blacksburg for six months, and Mom and Dad came for a visit.

> They saw we were doing well.
> The house was good.
> We had working vehicles.
> Groceries were in the pantry.
> The refrigerator was full.

Mom and Dad saw that we had moved a thousand miles away and had done well.

Later that evening, after we treated them to a steak dinner, Dad looked at me and said, "Well, I can die peacefully. My kids are okay."

"Dad? What? Are you dying?"

> "No, son. I mean, my job is done. You and Baby Girl have landed on your feet and done well. My job as a father is complete."

I've never forgotten that conversation.

In his mind, certain criteria had to be met to let him know he had done well as a Dad.

On this day, in Blacksburg, Virginia, Dad was able to settle his heart that he had been a good father.

As a leader, what are the criteria you've set for yourself that you've succeeded?

Is it that the organization stays financially solvent as long as you're in the chair?

> Is it that you raise a generation of leaders?

Perhaps you'll know when you have to expand the mission and vision.

Maybe it's a combination of all of those.

> But how will you know you've done well?

Dad knew.

At that moment, on that day, he realized he was a great father.

Be like Dad...exceed the goals you've set for yourself.

One more thing....
Dad, you didn't just do well — you did great.

50. LEAVE A LEGACY

"Son, do you want to go to town with me?"

"I have to go and get some deer meat from Julio's. Want to ride with me?"

"Hey boy, want to hit the river and see if those striped bass are schooling?"

"Want to take a ride over to Calvin to your Grandpa's old place?"

"I'm riding over to my deer stand. Want to come see it?"

Dad was intentional in doing things with me.

He didn't invite me along because I was his son.

He did it because he enjoyed my company.

Yes, my Dad loved me.

There has never been a day in my life when I ever doubted that he loved me.

He never forced me to do anything.

I loved spending time with him.

His stories.

The jokes.

His laugh that could be heard two streets over.

His growl that was worse than his bite.

I miss him.

But I'm thankful that he wanted to spend time with me.

Want to be a better leader?

Spend time with your team.

Be intentional about it.
Don't just talk about work.
Be human.
Laugh.
Tell jokes.
Talk about life.

Do that, and you'll build trust with your team.

Also, do those things, and you'll leave a legacy of your influence in the lives of others.

Be like Dad…spend time with others. Make memories. Leave a legacy.

AFTERWORD

Dear Reader,

It still seems odd to refer to my Dad in the past tense.

I think I've said that two or three times in this short little book.

There are so many more stories I could share about my Dad.

Some would make you laugh, others would make you gasp, and a few might leave you in shock.

To convey what my Dad taught me in fifty short chapters was a difficult task.

Choosing which stories to use, how to convey them, and making sure they land correctly on the heart was not an easy undertaking.

Also, this book has been a labor of emotions.

Dad is gone.

Grief is something you never truly get over. It's something you build a new life around.

Writing this book was a step toward that for me.

I know I'm partial, and everyone is, but my Dad was the greatest.

I miss his phone calls when he would yell in the phone because somewhere in his mind, he thought that because we lived a thousand miles away, he had to talk louder.

His texts of fish he'd caught or deer he killed are things I'll never get again.

Being able to ask his advice about life, dealing with people, home repairs, and LSU football are a few of the things I truly miss.

On multiple occasions, I have reached for my phone to call him only to realize he would not answer.

It's then that grief overwhelms me like a tidal wave.

However, there is hope.

Dad knew Jesus, and Jesus knew my Dad.

In the last two months of Dad's life, the change was overwhelmingly transparent.

Just about everyone who visited or called, he'd ask them to forgive him of any wrong he had ever done to them.

He prayed a good bit.

Gentleness and kindness became a hallmark for him, and the tough-guy routine seemed to fade.

Dad would tell us repeatedly how much he loved us.

When Dad called to tell us the diagnosis and timeline, we all cried and chatted.

I remember saying, "Dad, cancer doesn't mean Jesus has abandoned you."

In his bellowing voice, he said, "Son, I know that. I know He loves me and has saved me. It just means I have cancer, and it doesn't look good."

He had a simple but strong faith.

I'm envious of that.

I was in the hospital room on the night Dad died.

All I can say is that when Dad left, an indescribable peace overtook that room.

Yes, I was sad and crying, but there was peace and calm.

I told my pastor this, and he said, "That peace you experienced was Jesus coming to claim one of His own."

Pastor Chris was right.

Dad knew Jesus, and Jesus knew my Dad.

Granted, Dad may have come across a little more like John Wayne than he did Jesus, but he still knew Him.

(Thanks to Bill Gaither for that analogy.)

Miss ya, Dad.

Love ya.

And to the person holding this book, thank you for taking the time to read about my Dad.

I pray some of what he taught me is now a part of you.

Brian

ABOUT THE AUTHOR

Brian Sanders is passionate about leadership. Serving as the Executive Vice-President of Positive Alternative Radio, he leads the team that runs five of the most award-winning and fastest-growing Christian radio stations in America.

Brian is a prolific writer. His recent book, *Leadership Endurance*, hit #1 on Amazon's Christian Leadership Best Seller List and is now in its third printing. The book draws inspiration from God's Word, as well as some of the greatest leaders of all time, including Lincoln, Grant, Churchill, and Franklin Delano Roosevelt.

Brian's true heart is for leaders who feel overwhelmed and not worthy of their calling.

> "As a large man with a speech impediment, I've gone through a lot to get where I am," Brian says. "God uses flawed people to accomplish great things."

Brian lives in the Blue Ridge Mountains of Virginia with his wife, Kayla. He holds a bachelor's degree from Northwestern State University in Louisiana. He has fifty-nine hours toward a Master of Divinity from New Orleans Baptist Theological Seminary. You can often find him reading a book, coaching leaders, or telling a story about Abraham Lincoln.

To contact Brian, you may email him at Brian@briansandersauthor.com.

Brian's website is www.briansandersauthor.com.

#1 AMAZON BEST SELLER: CHRISTIAN LEADERSHIP

AVAILABLE:
BRIANSANDERSAUTHOR.COM AND AMAZON.COM

ACKNOWLEDGMENTS

This book wouldn't be possible without the support of so many people.

To Mrs. Kayla – thank you for your love and encouragement throughout this entire process.

To my editors, Donna Carpenter, Susan Greenwood, and Rhonda Lacey – you make me a better writer.

To Susan Greenwood for the countless hours formatting and layout this book.

To the promotional team, Cassie Conley, Doug Day, Zac Myers, and Adam Read — thanks to your efforts, people will actually know about this book.

To Matt Billingsley who designed and created so much with this book — you make me look good!

To Jerry Grimes who shepherded the entire project — thank you, sir. I couldn't have done this without you.

To Edward Baker, the President of Positive Alternative Radio — thanks for believing in me and this project.

To the entire team at Positive Alternative Radio — thanks for allowing me to share with you the wisdom that my Dad gave me.

Finally, to Jesus – thank you for giving me the best Dad that has ever walked this earth.